Good Housekeeping Cookery Club

TRADITIONAL BRITISH COOKING

Joanna Farrow

EBURY PRESS
LONDON

First published 1995

1 3 5 7 9 10 8 6 4 2

First published in the United Kingdom in 1995 by
Ebury Press, Random House, 20 Vauxhall Bridge Road, London SW1V 2SA

Random House Australia (Pty) Limited
20 Alfred Street, Milsons Point, Sydney,
New South Wales 2061, Australia

Random House New Zealand Limited
18 Poland Road, Glenfield,
Auckland 10, New Zealand

Random House South Africa (Pty) Limited
PO Box 337, Bergvlei, South Africa

Random House UK Limited Reg. No. 954009

A CIP catalogue record for this book is available from the British Library.

Managing Editor: JANET ILLSLEY
Design: SARA KIDD
Special Photography: GRAHAM KIRK
Food Stylist: JOANNA FARROW
Photographic Stylist: HELEN PAYNE
Techniques Photography: KARL ADAMSON
Food Techniques Stylist: ANGELA KINGSBURY
Recipe Testing: EMMA-LEE GOW

ISBN 0 09 180899 5

Typeset in Gill Sans by Textype Typesetters, Cambridge
Colour Separations by Magnacraft, London
Printed and bound in Italy by New Interlitho Italia S.p.a., Milan

CONTENTS

COOKERY NOTES

- Both metric and imperial measures are given for the recipes. Follow either metric or imperial throughout as they are not interchangeable.
- All spoon measures are level unless otherwise stated. Sets of measuring spoons are available in metric and imperial for accurate measurement of small quantities.
- Ovens should be preheated to the specified temperature. Grills should also be preheated. The cooking times given in the recipes assume that this has been done.

- Where a stage is specified under freezing, the dish should be frozen at the end of that stage.
- Size 2 eggs should be used except where otherwise specified. Free-range eggs are recommended.
- Use freshly ground black pepper and sea salt unless otherwise specified.
- Use fresh rather than dried herbs unless dried herbs are suggested in the recipe.
- Stocks should be freshly made if possible. Alternatively buy ready-made stocks or good quality stock cubes.

INTRODUCTION

Succulent roasts, rich nourishing soups, warming pies and stews, and sweet sticky puddings... these are just a few of the great British favourites. We still have a deep nostalgia for these traditional dishes, although our love of foreign flavours has seduced us away from the best of British food.

Thankfully, however, in recent years there has been a revival of traditional British cooking. This may be partly due to our tiring with over-complicated and pretentious food, but it probably owes more to a new generation of successful, down-to-earth chefs, who have revitalised British cooking methods and flavour combinations to give our best-loved foods fresh new flavours and appeal.

This collection of recipes is a celebration of great British dishes, many of which I have adapted to suit today's tastes and lifestyles.

Lengthy steaming and boiling give way to faster cooking methods, so that foods retain more colour and texture. Additional 'extras' have been added to bring out well-loved flavours and in some cases an innovative 'twist' gives a recipe a new lease of life.

With some recipes, of course, little can be done to improve a great classic. How could we possibly interfere with a comforting Pea and Ham Soup, a steaming hot Steak and Kidney Pudding, or a deep and delicious Treacle Tart?

Defining exactly 'what is traditional' is not easy. Over the centuries, British cooking has been influenced by so many 'foreign' ingredients, cooking techniques and eating styles, that some have become an intrinsic part of our own culinary heritage. For example, the custom of beginning a meal with a starter is comparatively recent. Originally soup or pottage – rich with meat and vegetables – was only served as a main meal with plenty of potatoes or bread.

Here I have included a few favourite soups, with modified proportions, so that they can be served as starters. But, of course, they make wonderful main courses too!

The splendid range of fish available from our rivers and seas lends itself to a variety of excellent dishes. Try plain, simple fish cakes – deliciously updated by combining mackerel and fennel in a crisp oatmeal crumb – accompanied by a gooseberry butter sauce. For a special occasion, bake a whole sea bass to perfection and complement it with an orangey saffron sauce.

With the meat, poultry and game dishes, there's room for modernisation too. For example, pease pudding is lightly whipped with herbs and olive oil, then grilled... to delicious effect.

For many of us puddings are what British food is all about, and many of those featured in this collection are based on real classics. Perhaps the 'oldest' is Syllabub, which evolved from the custom of topping ale with fresh, foaming cow's milk, to give a creamy head over an alcoholic base.

I hope this collection of updated traditional recipes will encourage you to 'cook British' for your family and friends. After all we have a style of cooking of which we can justly be proud, and above all enjoy!

PREPARATION TECHNIQUES

Many of the recipes in this book use the same basic techniques, whether it's to make stocks, sauces, meat, fish or pastries. On the following pages are some step-by-step guides that will help to clarify the techniques used in the recipes.

STOCKS AND SAUCES

For soups, stews and gravies, a homemade stock makes a far tastier base than stock cubes, particularly if you obtain fresh bones from the butcher. If the bones are already cooked, omit the browning stage. If not required for immediate use, stock can be frozen for a later date.

MAKING STOCK

1. Put the meat bones in a roasting tin and cook in a preheated oven at 230°C (450°F) Mark 8 for about 40 minutes until browned.

2. Transfer the bones to a large saucepan. Add a halved, unpeeled onion, 2 roughly chopped carrots, 1 halved stick of celery, 2 bay leaves, a sprinkling of black peppercorns and some fresh herbs if liked. Cover with cold water and bring slowly to the boil.

3. Skim off any scum using a slotted spoon. Reduce the heat and simmer very gently, allowing 2 hours for chicken and poultry; 3-4 hours for red meats. Leave to cool and then strain.

NOTE: For fish stock, omit the browning and use a peeled onion. Add 1-2 parsley sprigs and a strip of lemon rind and simmer for 20-30 minutes. Strain through a fine sieve.

MAKING A WHITE SAUCE

1. Melt the butter in a saucepan. Blend in the flour and cook, stirring, for 1 minute to make a paste.

2. Remove from the heat and gradually blend in the milk until completely smooth, whisking constantly.

3. Return to the heat and cook over a gentle heat, whisking constantly, until the sauce is thickened and smooth. Add cheese, herbs, or other flavourings, and seasoning.

MAKING GRAVY

1. Using a large metal spoon, skim almost all of the fat from the roasting tin, leaving the meat juices.

2. Add a little flour to the juices and stir until no lumps remain.

3. Gradually pour in the stock, or half stock and half wine, stirring and scraping up the pan residue. Slowly bring to the boil and bubble for 2-3 minutes. Season to taste.

NOTE: For a thinner gravy, omit flour and boil to thicken slightly.

MAKING CUSTARD

This is the recipe used to make a 'real' custard. It also forms the basis of several creamy desserts.

3 egg yolks
30 ml (2 tbsp) caster sugar
2.5 ml (½ tsp) cornflour
300 ml (½ pint) milk
2.5 ml (½ tsp) vanilla essence
(optional)

1. Place the egg yolks, sugar and cornflour in a bowl with a little of the milk and whisk until smooth.

2. Bring the milk to the boil in a heavy-based saucepan. Pour the milk onto the egg yolk mixture, whisking well. Return to the saucepan and add a little vanilla essence, if liked.

3. Cook over the lowest possible heat, stirring constantly, for about 10 minutes until the custard thickens slightly. It should be thick enough to thinly coat the back of the wooden spoon. Do not boil or the custard may curdle. Strain and serve.

NOTE: A traditional egg custard doesn't include cornflour, but you will find that incorporating a little greatly reduces the risk of curdling.

SEARING

This technique is applied to meat to quickly brown and seal it before stewing or roasting.

1. To sear a whole joint of meat or a chicken or duck, pat dry on kitchen paper.

2. Heat the oil in a frying pan. Add the meat and fry on all sides, gradually turning the meat until seared all over.

1. For small pieces of meat, thoroughly pat dry on kitchen paper. Season flour with salt and pepper and use to coat the meat pieces.

2. Heat the oil in the frying pan and fry off the meat in batches. Avoid adding too much to the pan in one go otherwise it will steam rather than brown.

SHALLOW-FRYING

1. Pour a little vegetable oil into a frying pan to a depth of about 5 mm (¼ inch). Heat until a piece of bread or batter sizzles as soon as it is added to the pan.

2. Add the fish or fish cakes to the hot oil and fry gently, turning carefully when golden on the underside.

DEEP-FRYING

1. Half-fill a deep saucepan or deep-fat fryer with vegetable oil and heat to 190°C (375°F). Fry a few pieces at a time, then drain on kitchen paper. Do not overfill the pan with fish otherwise it won't cook properly.

SKINNING FISH

Lay the fish fillet, skin-side down with the tail end towards you. Dip the fingers of one hand in salt to help grip the fish. Hold a filleting knife against the skin with the blade almost parallel to it, and push away from you using a sawing action.

TESTING COOKED FISH

Fish cooking times vary according to the thickness of the fish, the temperature it started at and the degree of heat. Test fish towards the end of the stated cooking time.

Pierce the thickest area of the fish with the tip of a fine-bladed knife. The colour should be just opaque and the flesh flaking apart.

COOKING IN A WATER BATH

1. Stand the pâté dish, ramekins or individual pudding basins in a deep-sided roasted tin.

2. Pour boiling water into the tin until it comes about a third or half-way up the sides of the dish.

3. Cover completely with foil and carefully transfer to the oven using oven gloves.

COVERING A PIE DISH

1. Roll out the pastry thinly until it is about 5 cm (2 inches) larger than the pie dish all round. Cut a 2.5 cm (1 inch) strip from the outside of the pastry.

SUETCRUST PASTRY

2. Place this strip on the moistened rim of the pie dish. Brush the pastry strip with water.

5. Using a sharp knife, trim off the excess pastry.

1. Add the suet to the sifted flour and stir to combine. Add enough cold water to make a slightly sticky dough, mixing with a round-bladed knife.

3. Lift the pastry lid into position.

6. Knock up the edges of the pastry to create a flaky appearance.

2. Turn the dough out onto a floured surface and knead lightly if using for pastry.

4. Press the edges of the pastry together to seal.

7. Press your thumb on the rim of the pastry and gently draw the blade of a knife towards the centre. Repeat at 2.5 cm (1 inch) intervals.

3. If shaping dumplings, divide the dough into even-sized pieces and roll into balls with floured hands.

COCK-A-LEEKIE

Tender, shredded chicken, pungent leeks and sweet, juicy prunes make a wonderful threesome in this classic Scottish dish. Originally cheap cuts of beef were often used to make a rich stock, but now a light chicken stock is more acceptable. Serve topped with the baby dumplings as a hearty starter, or without, if there's plenty to follow. As a main course, this soup will serve 4.

SERVES 8

1.4 kg (3 lb) oven-ready
   chicken
2 onions
2 carrots
2 celery sticks
I bay leaf
900 g (2 lb) leeks
25 g (I oz) butter
125 g (4 oz) ready-to-eat
   pitted prunes
salt and freshly ground black
   pepper
DUMPLINGS
125 g (4 oz) self-raising
   white flour
pinch of salt
50 g (2 oz) shredded suet
30 ml (2 tbsp) chopped fresh
   parsley
30 ml (2 tbsp) chopped fresh
   thyme
TO GARNISH
parsley and thyme sprigs

PREPARATION TIME
20 minutes
COOKING TIME
I hour 20 minutes
FREEZING
Not suitable

250 CALS PER SERVING

1. Peel and roughly chop the onions and carrots. Roughly chop the celery. Place the chicken in a saucepan in which it fits quite snugly. Add the chopped vegetables, bay leaf and chicken giblets (if available). Add 1.8 litres (3 pints) water. Bring to the boil, reduce the heat, cover and simmer gently for I hour.

2. Trim and slice the leeks. Melt the butter in a large saucepan, add the leeks and fry gently for 10 minutes. Slice the prunes.

3. Remove the chicken from the pan; strain the stock and set aside. Remove the chicken from the bones and roughly shred. Add to the stock with the prunes and leeks.

4. For the dumplings, sift the flour and salt into a bowl. Stir in the suet, herbs and about 75 ml (5 tbsp) water to make a fairly firm dough. Shape the dough into 2.5 cm (I inch) balls.

5. Bring the soup just to the boil and season with salt and pepper to taste. Reduce the heat, add the dumplings and cover with a lid. Simmer for about 15-20 minutes until the dumplings are light and fluffy. Serve hot, garnished with the herbs.

NOTE: If possible, make the stock the day before required; allow to cool then refrigerate overnight. The next day, remove any fat from the surface.

TECHNIQUE

Shape the dough into 2.5 cm (I inch) balls for the dumplings.

PEA AND HAM SOUP

A meaty smoked bacon knuckle, given long gentle simmering, makes a deliciously rich base for this well-loved, robust soup. Spoonfuls of crème fraîche, added to each serving, provide a refreshing contrast. Don't forget to soften the dried green peas by soaking overnight before cooking with the meat. As a warming wintry main course, accompanied by plenty of crusty bread, this soup will serve 4.

SERVES 8

450 g (1 lb) dried split or
    whole green peas
1-1.1 kg (2¼-2½ lb) smoked
    bacon knuckle
2 large onions
2 carrots
2 celery sticks
2 bay leaves
salt and pepper
TO SERVE
150 ml (¼ pint) crème
    fraîche
flat-leaved parsley, to
    garnish

PREPARATION TIME
15 minutes, plus overnight
soaking
COOKING TIME
1¾ hours
FREEZING
Suitable

340 CALS PER SERVING

1. Put the dried peas in a large bowl and cover with plenty of cold water. Leave to soak overnight.

2. Place the bacon in a large saucepan and add sufficient cold water to cover. Bring slowly to the boil, then drain and return to the clean pan. Drain the peas and add to the pan.

3. Peel and roughly chop the onions. Peel and roughly slice the carrots. Cut the celery into chunks. Add to the pan with the bay leaves. Cover with cold water and bring to the boil.

4. Reduce the heat and cover with a lid. Simmer very gently for 1½ hours until the bacon and peas are very tender. Discard the bay leaves.

5. Lift the bacon from the pan. Cut into chunks, discarding the skin and bones, then chop finely.

6. Purée the soup in a blender or food processor until smooth, then place in a clean pan with the chopped meat. Heat through gently, adding a little stock if the soup is very thick. Season with a little salt if necessary, and pepper to taste.

7. Ladle the soup into warmed individual serving bowls and add a generous swirl of crème fraîche to each bowl. Serve garnished with roughly torn parsley.

NOTE: Use a blender in preference to a food processor for puréeing the soup as it gives a smoother result.

VARIATIONS

Use yellow split peas instead of green ones, cooking them in the same way.

TECHNIQUE

Remove the lean meat from the knuckle, discarding the skin and bone.

COCKLE AND POTATO CHOWDER

In this delicious recipe, cooked cockles and creamy, floury potatoes are warmed with a hint of saffron, coriander, orange and thyme. Serve this hearty soup as a substantial starter, or tuck into it as a main meal with plenty of grainy bread. As a main course this quantity will serve 4.

SERVES 6

2 carrots

2 onions

1 celery stick

10 ml (2 tsp) coriander seeds

25 g (1 oz) butter

2 bay leaves

2 thyme sprigs

1 strip pared orange rind

2.5 ml (½ tsp) saffron strands

450 g (1 lb) cooked cockles, thoroughly drained

600 ml (1 pint) milk

450 ml (¾ pint) fish stock or water

700 g (1½ lb) floury potatoes

salt and pepper

TO SERVE

60 ml (4 tbsp) double cream

thyme sprigs

PREPARATION TIME
15 minutes
COOKING TIME
25 minutes
FREEZING
Not suitable

285 CALS PER SERVING

1. Peel and roughly dice the carrots. Peel and chop the onions. Roughly chop the celery. Crush the coriander seeds with a pestle and mortar.

2. Melt the butter in a large saucepan. Add the carrots, onions and celery and fry gently for 5 minutes. Stir in the coriander seeds, bay leaves, thyme, orange rind, saffron, cockles, milk and fish stock.

3. Peel and cut the potatoes into small dice, then add to the pan. Bring slowly to the boil, then reduce the heat and cover with a lid. Cook gently for 15-20 minutes until the potatoes are tender. Discard the bay leaves, thyme and orange rind.

4. Transfer half of the soup to a blender or food processor and work until smooth. Return to the saucepan and season with salt and pepper to taste.

5. Ladle into warmed soup bowls and swirl each with a little cream. Sprinkle with small sprigs of thyme.

NOTE: Fresh cockles in their shells are generally difficult to get hold of. If you manage to obtain some, prepare as for mussels, first scrubbing, then cooking briefly in a pan with water; discard any that do not open.

VARIATIONS

● Use cooked, shelled mussels instead of cockles.

● Replace the cockles with smoked haddock. Remove the skin and any bones from the fish before adding to the pan.

TECHNIQUE

Blend half of the soup in a blender or food processor until smooth, then combine with the rest of the soup.

FRESH SALMON MOUSSES

These loosely wrapped parcels of fresh and smoked salmon make an excellent prepare-ahead starter, whatever the occasion. Lightly poached fresh salmon is puréed, lightened with whipped cream and softly set before scooping and enveloping in slices of smoked salmon. A little fresh chives or tarragon adds a delicate flavouring, although fresh dill makes an equally good alternative.

SERVES 8

450 g (1 lb) salmon tail or cutlets

1 carrot

1 onion

1 bay leaf

150 ml (¼ pint) fish stock

salt and pepper

7.5 ml (1½ tsp) powdered gelatine

75 ml (3 fl oz) dry white wine

15 ml (1 tbsp) chopped fresh chives or tarragon

45 ml (3 tbsp) mayonnaise

150 ml (¼ pint) double cream

8 slices smoked salmon, about 175 g (6 oz) total weight

TO GARNISH

quail's eggs

fish eggs (optional)

tarragon sprigs

PREPARATION TIME
35 minutes, plus setting
COOKING TIME
About 12 minutes
FREEZING
Not suitable

270 CALS PER SERVING

1. Place the salmon in a pan in which it fits quite snugly. Peel and roughly chop the carrot and onion. Add to the pan with the bay leaf, stock and seasoning. Bring to the boil, reduce the heat and simmer very gently for 10 minutes, turning the salmon halfway through cooking.

2. Drain the fish, reserving the stock. Pull the flesh away from the bone, then roughly flake the fish, discarding the skin and any stray bones. Strain the stock and set aside.

3. Sprinkle the gelatine over the white wine in a small heatproof bowl and leave to soften for 5 minutes.

4. Meanwhile, blend the fish in a food processor with the cooking juices until almost smooth. Transfer to a bowl.

5. Stand the bowl of gelatine in a pan of simmering water and leave until dissolved. Stir into the salmon mixture, then beat in the chives or tarragon and mayonnaise; season lightly.

6. Lightly whip the cream until just holding its shape. Fold into the salmon mixture, using a large metal spoon. Turn the mousse into a container and chill for several hours or overnight until softly set.

7. To serve, lay the smoked salmon slices on a board. Place a spoonful of the mousse on each slice. Bring the ends of the salmon up over the mousse and twist together. Arrange on individual serving plates and garnish with quail's eggs, fish eggs and tarragon sprigs.

NOTE: If making the mousse a day in advance reduce the amount of gelatine to 5 ml (1 tsp) so that it does not set too firmly.

VARIATIONS

● Use trout fillets instead of the salmon.
● For added texture, fold some chopped prawns into the mousse with the cream.

TECHNIQUE

Spoon the mousse onto the smoked salmon slices. Bring the smoked salmon up over the top and twist gently to secure.

CHUNKY PATÉ WITH PORT AND PISTACHIOS

Chunky pieces of pork, duck, bacon, chicken and chicken livers are mixed together in this easily made, yet richly flavoured pâté. Once cooked the meat juices are mixed with port or sherry and set around the pâté to seal in the flavour and enhance presentation. Store in the refrigerator for up to 2 days and serve individual portions scooped onto a bed of salad leaves.

SERVES 8

350 g (12 oz) boneless belly pork

1 large chicken breast

1 large duck breast

125 g (4 oz) streaky bacon, derinded

225 g (8 oz) chicken livers, trimmed

45 ml (3 tbsp) white or red port, or brandy

5 ml (1 tsp) salt

black pepper

15 ml (1 tbsp) chopped fresh rosemary

40 g (1½ oz) shelled pistachio nuts

TO FINISH

few bay leaves

several rosemary sprigs

10 ml (2 tsp) powdered gelatine

150 ml (¼ pint) white port or dry sherry

PREPARATION TIME
25 minutes, plus setting
COOKING TIME
About 1½ hours
FREEZING
Not suitable

325 CALS PER SERVING

1. Preheat the oven to 160°C (325°F) Mark 3. Remove any rind from the belly pork, then roughly chop. Place in a food processor and mince coarsely, retaining some small chunks. Remove the skin from the chicken breast, then mince in the processor. Skin the duck breast and chop into small pieces. Dice the bacon. Wash and mince the chicken livers.

2. Mix together all the meats in a large bowl. Add the port or brandy, salt, pepper, rosemary and nuts. Mix together until evenly combined.

3. Pack the mixture into a 1.1 litre (2 pint) terrine or ovenproof dish. Stand the dish in a roasting tin and pour boiling water into the tin to a depth of 2.5 cm (1 inch). Cover with foil and bake in the oven for 1 hour.

4. Remove the foil and arrange the herbs over the pâté. Cook for a further 30 minutes until the juices run clear when pierced with a skewer.

5. Drain the meat juices into a small heatproof bowl and leave to cool.

6. Skim any fat from the meat juices, then sprinkle over the gelatine and leave for 5 minutes until softened. Stand the

bowl in a little simmering water and leave until dissolved. Pour the port or sherry into the juices, stirring well. Measure the liquid and make up to 450 ml (¾ pint) with water, if necessary.

7. Pour the liquid over the pâté and chill until it has set. Serve with warm bread and salad.

NOTE: If preferred, cook the pâté in ramekins or dariole moulds, reducing the cooking time to about 45 minutes.

VARIATION

Replace the pistachio nuts with 30 ml (2 tbsp) pink or green peppercorns.

TECHNIQUE

Carefully pour the gelatine mixture around the cooled pâté until covered with a thin layer.

POTTED MIXED SEAFOOD WITH HERB SODA BREAD

Sweet, meaty prawns are flavoured with a hint of garlic, and packed into little pots with moist flakes of poached trout. Serve the accompanying soda bread very fresh – preferably still warm from the oven.

SERVES 8

POTTED SEAFOOD
2 large trout
300 g (10 oz) lightly salted butter
700 g (1½ lb) large raw prawns (see note)
2 garlic cloves, crushed
1.25 ml (¼ tsp) ground mace
pepper
SODA BREAD
600 ml (1 pint) milk
15 ml (1 tbsp) lemon juice
225 g (8 oz) plain wholemeal flour
375 g (13 oz) strong white flour
10 ml (2 tsp) salt
5 ml (1 tsp) bicarbonate of soda
25 g (1 oz) butter
1 spring onion, chopped
45 ml (3 tbsp) chopped herbs (parsley, tarragon, chervil)
50 g (2 oz) medium oatmeal
extra oatmeal, for sprinkling

PREPARATION TIME
35 minutes, plus chilling
COOKING TIME
Potted Seafood: 20 minutes; Bread 25 minutes
FREEZING Not suitable

720 CALS PER SERVING`

---

1. To make the potted seafood, wrap the trout in buttered foil, seal tightly and lower into a saucepan containing 2.5 cm (1 inch) depth of boiling water. Cover and steam for about 20 minutes until the thickest area of the fish flakes easily. Remove and leave to cool.

2. Flake the trout into small pieces, discarding skin and bones. Heat 50 g (2 oz) butter in a frying pan. Add the prawns with the garlic and mace; cook for 2 minutes until pink on the underside. Turn and cook for a further 1-2 minutes until pink all over. Remove with a slotted spoon, reserving the butter in the pan.

3. Peel the prawns and pack with the trout into 8 small ramekins. Cut the remaining butter into pieces and add to the pan. Stir until melted and add a little pepper.

4. Turn the melted butter into a jug and pour over the ramekins until the fish is just submerged. Leave to cool, then chill for several hours until firm.

5. For the soda bread, preheat the oven to 220°C (425°F) Mark 7. Mix together the milk and lemon juice. Sift the flours, salt and bicarbonate of soda into a bowl, adding any bran left in the sieve. Rub in the butter. Add the spring onion, herbs and oatmeal.

6. Add most of the milk and mix to a dough with a round-bladed knife, adding the remaining milk as necessary. Turn out onto a floured surface and knead lightly.

7. Divide the mixture in half and shape each piece into a round. Place slightly apart on a lightly greased large baking sheet. Score with the back of a knife, then sprinkle generously with oatmeal. Bake for about 25 minutes until risen and browned. Transfer to a wire rack.

8. Loosen the potted seafood and turn out onto serving plates. Surround with a herb salad and serve with the warm soda bread.

NOTE: If raw prawns are unobtainable, use 575 g (1¼ lb) cooked shelled prawns instead. Heat through for 1 minute only.

TECHNIQUE

Pour the melted butter over the fish in each ramekin until just covered.

SMOKED HAM AND EGGS ON MUSTARD MUFFINS

Freshly cooked muffins, crispy cased with a steaming, airy centre, are a time-honoured treat that no supermarket can successfully imitate. These ones are split and topped with smoked ham and poached eggs, and blanketed under a lemony Hollandaise for a mouth-watering lunch or supper dish.

SERVES 4

MUFFINS

175 g (6 oz) strong plain white flour

2.5 ml (½ tsp) fast-action dried yeast

2.5 ml (½ tsp) caster sugar

1.25 ml (¼ tsp) salt

10 ml (2 tsp) grainy English mustard

15 g (½ oz) butter, melted

flour, for dusting

a little oil, for frying

SAUCE

75 g (3 oz) lightly salted butter

5 ml (1 tsp) lemon juice

finely grated rind of ½ lemon

2 egg yolks

pepper

TO FINISH

dash of vinegar

4 eggs

4 thin slices smoked ham

chervil sprigs, to garnish

PREPARATION TIME
30 minutes, plus rising
COOKING TIME
About 20 minutes
FREEZING
Suitable: Muffins only

550 CALS PER SERVING

1. To make the muffins, sift the flour into a bowl and stir in the yeast, sugar and salt. Mix together the mustard, melted butter and 150 ml (¼ pint) water and add to the bowl. Mix well to make a fairly soft dough.

2. Turn out onto a floured surface and knead for 10 minutes. Place in an oiled bowl, cover and leave to rise for about 1 hour until doubled in size.

3. Turn the dough out onto a floured surface and knead lightly. Divide into four and shape each piece into a round. Place on a lightly greased baking sheet, cover with a damp tea-towel and leave to rise for about 30 minutes.

4. Brush a heavy-based frying pan with oil and place over a moderate heat. Dust the muffins with flour. Slide off the baking sheet on a fish slice and invert into the pan. Fry gently for about 10 minutes on each side until crisp. Remove from the pan and keep warm.

5. For the sauce, cut the butter into small pieces. Place the lemon juice, rind and egg yolks in a heatproof bowl over a pan of simmering water. Gradually whisk in the butter until smooth. If too thick, add a little warm water. Season with pepper; keep warm.

6. Heat a saucepan of water and add the vinegar. Break the eggs into the pan and simmer gently for about 3 minutes until cooked through.

7. Meanwhile, split the muffins. Arrange the bases on warmed serving plates and cover with the ham slices. Carefully lift the eggs out of the pan, drain well and place one on each serving. Spoon over the sauce and position the muffin tops. Serve garnished with chervil.

NOTE: If the sauce overheats and starts to curdle, add a dash of warm water and beat well. If this fails, start again with a fresh egg, gradually whisking in the curdled mixture.

TECHNIQUE

Slide a fish slice under the muffins and invert them into the heated frying pan.

CHEESE AND APPLE PARCELS

Tangy Cheshire cheese and sweet, juicy apple are simply wrapped in buttery morsels of melting puff pastry. To save time, you can of course buy ready-made puff pastry rather than make your own. Serve the pastries on a bed of lightly dressed herb and leaf salad, as a light lunch or supper.

MAKES 10

PASTRY

175 g (6 oz) firm unsalted butter

225 g (8 oz) plain white flour

pinch of salt

5 ml (1 tsp) lemon juice

FILLING

125 g (4 oz) Cheshire cheese

1 large dessert apple

45 ml (3 tbsp) chopped fresh parsley

salt and pepper

beaten egg, to glaze

TO SERVE

salad leaves

PREPARATION TIME
35 minutes, plus chilling
COOKING TIME
About 15 minutes
FREEZING
Suitable: Stage 5

260 CALS PER PARCEL

1. To make the pastry, cut the butter into small dice. Sift the flour and salt into a bowl. Add the butter, lemon juice and 100 ml (3½ fl oz) very cold water. Using a round-bladed knife, mix to a soft dough, adding a little extra water if the mixture is too dry.

2. Knead lightly, then roll out on a lightly floured surface to an oblong, about 30 cm (12 inches) long and 10 cm (4 inches) wide. Fold the bottom third up and the lower third down, keeping the edges straight, then give the pastry a quarter turn. Repeat the rolling, folding and turning four more times. Wrap in greaseproof paper and leave to rest in the refrigerator for at least 30 minutes.

3. For the filling, crumble the cheese into a bowl. Peel, core and quarter the apple, then cut into small dice. Add to the bowl with the parsley and seasoning.

4. Preheat the oven to 220°C (425°F) Mark 7. Roll out half the pastry thinly on a lightly floured surface and cut out five 12 cm (5 inch) rounds, using a small saucer or bowl as a guide.

5. Brush the edges of the circles with beaten egg, then spoon a little filling onto one side of each of the rounds. Fold the other half over the filling and press the edges together well to seal. Lightly flute the edges.

6. Transfer the pastries to a lightly greased baking sheet and brush with beaten egg. Score each pastry several times across the top. Use the remaining pastry and filling to make five more parcels in the same way. Bake for about 15 minutes until risen and golden. Serve warm with a lightly dressed salad.

TECHNIQUE

Bring the pastry over the filling to enclose, pressing the edges together firmly to seal.

KEDGEREE WITH HERB BUTTER

This simple combination of basmati rice, lightly poached smoked haddock, boiled eggs and subtle spice, makes a lovely combination that's perfect for a light lunch, or more traditionally a breakfast dish to set you up for the day! The cockles and lemony herb butter provide additional flavour. As a more substantial main course this recipe will serve 2-3.

SERVES 4

450 g (1 lb) smoked haddock (see note)
150 ml (¼ pint) milk
75 g (3 oz) cooked cockles
5 ml (1 tsp) coriander seeds
3 hard-boiled eggs
225 g (8 oz) basmati rice
30 ml (2 tbsp) double cream
45-60 ml (3-4 tbsp) chopped fresh chives
salt and pepper
HERB BUTTER
50 g (2 oz) butter
5-10 ml (1-2 tsp) lemon juice
30 ml (2 tbsp) chopped fresh tarragon
TO GARNISH
lemon or lime wedges and extra herbs

PREPARATION TIME
10 minutes
COOKING TIME
About 20 minutes
FREEZING
Not suitable

540 CALS PER SERVING

1. Place the smoked haddock in a shallow pan with the milk. Cover and simmer gently for about 8 minutes until cooked through. Drain, reserving 30-45 ml (2-3 tbsp) of the juices. Roughly flake the fish, discarding the skin and any bones.

2. Thoroughly drain the cockles. Finely crush the coriander seeds. Shell and quarter the eggs.

3. Cook the rice in plenty of boiling, salted water for 10 minutes or until just tender. Drain, rinse with boiling water and drain well.

4. Return the rice to the pan and add the flaked haddock, reserved cooking juices, cockles, coriander seeds, quartered eggs, cream and chives. Season lightly with salt and pepper and heat through gently for 2 minutes.

5. Meanwhile, for the herb butter, melt the butter and stir in the lemon juice, tarragon and a little seasoning. Pour into a warmed jug.

6. Spoon the kedgeree onto warmed serving plates and garnish with lemon or lime wedges and extra herbs. Serve accompanied by the herb butter.

NOTE: Choose natural undyed smoked haddock where possible. It's very pale by comparison to the familiar yellow smoked haddock because it doesn't contain colouring and it generally has a superior flavour.

VARIATIONS

● Use fresh salmon instead of smoked haddock.
● Replace the tarragon in the herb butter with dill or chervil.

TECHNIQUE

Roughly flake the haddock fillets, discarding the skin and bone.

SEA BASS WITH SAFFRON AND ORANGE SAUCE

A whole fish makes a stunning centrepiece for a special meal, whether it's a winter celebration dinner or a summer lunch party. Here sea bass is simply baked with plenty of herbs and accompanied by a creamy orange sauce – fragrant and vibrant with saffron.

SERVES 6

75 g (3 oz) butter
I large sea bass, about
   1.4 kg (3 lb)
salt and pepper
handful of mixed herbs (eg
   tarragon, parsley, chervil)
SAUCE
2.5 ml (½ tsp) saffron
   strands
5 ml (I tsp) cornflour
300 ml (½ pint) double
   cream
finely grated rind of
   I orange
TO GARNISH
fresh herb sprigs
cooked whole prawns
   (optional)

PREPARATION TIME
25 minutes
COOKING TIME
40 minutes
FREEZING
Not suitable

550 CALS PER SERVING

1. Preheat the oven to 220°C (425°F) Mark 7. Lightly butter a large piece of foil and use to line a roasting tin large enough to hold the fish. Rub the fish inside and out with salt and pepper and place in the foil-lined tin. Tuck the herbs into the cavity and dot the remaining butter over the fish.

2. Cover the sea bass with foil and bake for about 40 minutes until the thickest area of the fish flakes easily when tested with a knife.

3. Meanwhile make the sauce. Crumble the saffron strands into a small bowl and add 30 ml (2 tbsp) hot water. Blend the cornflour with a little cold water in a small saucepan, then stir in the cream, grated orange rind and a little salt and pepper.

4. Add the saffron and liquid to the pan and cook, stirring, until slightly thickened. Simmer gently for 3 minutes.

5. Carefully lift the cooked bass from the roasting tin and invert the fish onto a board or clean work surface. Peel away the skin from the upper surface, then turn the bass onto a warmed serving platter. Remove the skin from the other side of the fish.

6. Garnish the fish lavishly with plenty of herbs, and cooked whole prawns, if desired. Serve accompanied by the warm saffron and orange sauce.

NOTE: If the bass won't fit comfortably in the tin, cut off the head and bake it beside the fish. Reposition the head when arranging on the serving plate.

VARIATIONS

Use a whole salmon or sea trout instead of sea bass.

TECHNIQUE

Tuck the herbs in the fish cavity, then dot the fish with the butter.

TROUT WITH CRISPY BACON AND ALMOND SAUCE

Fried trout with almonds is a recipe that's still commonly seen on many uninspiring restaurant menus. While this might taste pleasant if well cooked, it's nice to enjoy a more interesting variation on a well used theme. In this version the almonds are made into a delicious sauce with leeks, garlic, cream and ginger wine.

SERVES 4

4 small whole trout, gutted

8 thin rashers smoked
  streaky bacon

25 g (1 oz) butter

30 ml (2 tbsp) oil

25 g (1 oz) slivered almonds,
  toasted

SAUCE

½ small leek (green end)

25 g (1 oz) butter

2 garlic cloves, crushed

25 g (1 oz) ground almonds

60 ml (4 tbsp) ginger wine

45 ml (3 tbsp) double cream

salt and pepper

TO GARNISH

parsley sprigs

PREPARATION TIME
15 minutes
COOKING TIME
About 10 minutes
FREEZING
Not suitable

660 CALS PER SERVING

1. Lightly score the fish once or twice on each side. Wrap 2 rashers of bacon around each fish, securing in place with wooden cocktail sticks.

2. Melt the butter with the oil in a frying pan. Add the trout and fry gently for 5 minutes until the bacon is crisp and golden. Turn and fry for a further 5 minutes or until cooked through. Scatter the slivered almonds over the trout.

3. Meanwhile, trim and thinly slice the leek. Melt the butter in a saucepan. Add the leek and garlic and fry for 5 minutes until the leeks are softened.

4. Stir in the ground almonds and ginger wine and cook gently for 3 minutes until the mixture forms a soft paste. Stir in the cream and season with salt and pepper to taste.

5. Arrange the trout and almonds on warmed serving plates and add a generous spoonful of the sauce. Serve garnished with parsley.

NOTE: If short of space in the frying pan, cut off the fish heads before frying.

VARIATION

Use a medium sweet wine instead of the ginger wine.

TECHNIQUE

Wrap 2 rashers of bacon around each fish, securing in place with wooden cocktail sticks.

GRILLED HERRINGS WITH OATMEAL, SPINACH AND ALMONDS

Herrings are perfect for grilling – their oily, silvery skins turning beautifully crisp, charred and appetising. These herrings have a moist, tumbling spinach, almond and oatmeal stuffing, held together with a little melting Cheddar. For convenience they can be made a little in advance, ready for grilling at the last moment.

SERVES 4

4 herrings, boned
STUFFING
1 onion
125 g (4 oz) young spinach
　　leaves
25 g (1 oz) blanched
　　almonds
25 g (1 oz) butter
25 g (1 oz) medium oatmeal
75 g (3 oz) mature Cheddar
　　cheese, grated
salt and pepper
TO FINISH
10 ml (2 tsp) balsamic or
　　wine vinegar
lemon wedges, to serve

PREPARATION TIME
15 minutes
COOKING TIME
About 15 minutes
FREEZING
Not suitable

400 CALS PER SERVING

1. To make the stuffing, peel and finely chop the onion. Remove the tough stalks from the spinach. Chop the almonds. Melt the butter in a frying pan. Add the onion and almonds and fry for 3 minutes. Stir in the spinach and cook until just wilted.

2. Remove from the heat and stir in the oatmeal. Cool slightly, then add the cheese and a little seasoning.

3. Score the herrings, several times on each side. Sprinkle the balsamic vinegar inside the cavities and over the skins.

4. Spoon the prepared stuffing into the cavities and secure the opening with wooden cocktail sticks.

5. Preheat the grill to moderate. Lightly oil a sheet of foil and use to line a grill pan. Place the herrings in the pan and grill for 15 minutes, turning over, halfway through cooking.

6. Transfer the herrings to warmed serving plates and serve with lemon wedges and a tomato salad.

NOTE: If fresh spinach isn't available use 50 g (2 oz) frozen chopped spinach, thawing it thoroughly and squeezing out all excess moisture.

VARIATIONS

● Use pine nuts instead of chopped almonds.
● Use another hard cheese, such as Leicester or Gloucester, in place of Cheddar.

TECHNIQUE

Secure the herrings with cocktail sticks to hold in the stuffing.

SMOKED MACKEREL CAKES WITH GOOSEBERRY BUTTER

Fish cakes have recently seen a revival in popularity. This recipe uses the classic combination of mackerel and gooseberries. The mackerel cakes are enveloped in a crisp oatmeal crust and served with a tangy gooseberry sauce to cut the richness of the fish.

SERVES 4

SAUCE
175 g (6 oz) fresh or frozen
  gooseberries
50 g (2 oz) butter
25 g (1 oz) caster sugar
finely grated rind of
  ½ orange
FISH CAKES
450 g (1 lb) floury potatoes
salt and pepper
350 g (12 oz) smoked
  mackerel
1 large fennel bulb
50 g (2 oz) butter
1 egg yolk
60 ml (4 tbsp) chopped fresh
  chives
TO FINISH
50 g (2 oz) medium oatmeal
25 g (1 oz) breadcrumbs
1 egg white
oil for shallow-frying

PREPARATION TIME
30 minutes
COOKING TIME
About 10 minutes
FREEZING
Suitable: Fish cakes only

765 CALS PER SERVING

1. To make the sauce, trim the gooseberries. Melt the butter in a saucepan, add the gooseberries, sugar and orange rind, and cook gently until the gooseberries are pulpy. Beat lightly to break up the gooseberries. Reserve.

2. To make the fish cakes, peel the potatoes and cut into chunks. Cook in boiling salted water for 15 minutes or until tender. Drain well, then mash until smooth.

3. Discard the skin and any bones from the mackerel and flake the fish, using two forks. Trim and chop the fennel.

4. Melt the butter in a frying pan. Add the fennel and fry quickly until coloured. Transfer to a bowl and add the potatoes, mackerel, egg yolk and chives. Season with salt and pepper and divide the mixture into 8 portions.

5. Mix together the oatmeal and breadcrumbs on a plate. Lightly beat the egg white and pour onto another plate. Shape the fish portions into small round cakes. Dip each one in the egg white, then into the oatmeal mixture, turning to coat evenly.

6. Heat a 5 mm (¼ inch) depth of oil in a frying pan. Add half of the fish cakes and fry for 1-2 minutes until golden on the underside. Turn the fish cakes and cook for a further 1-2 minutes until crisp and golden. Drain on kitchen paper and keep warm while cooking the remainder.

7. Meanwhile, gently reheat the sauce. Serve the smoked mackerel cakes piping hot, accompanied by the sauce.

VARIATIONS

Use another oily fish, such as grilled herrings, instead of mackerel. Poached fresh or canned tuna, also works well.

TECHNIQUE

Dip the fish cakes in the egg white, then coat with the oatmeal mixture.

SALMON FILLETS IN PAPER WITH CHERVIL SAUCE

Cooking and serving fish in little paper parcels retains all the flavour and looks most attractive, particularly when the paper sears lightly with the heat of the oven. Serve the parcels slit open so that the sauce can be poured over the fish. Keep accompanying vegetables simple and serve as a light, summery supper or lunch.

SERVES 6

PARCELS

3 salmon tail fillets, each
   about 300 g (10 oz), or
   6 small salmon steaks

1 fennel bulb

25 g (1 oz) butter

1 lemon

20 ml (4 tsp) capers

30 ml (2 tbsp) roughly
   chopped chervil

salt and pepper

CHERVIL SAUCE

2.5 ml ($\frac{1}{2}$ tsp) cornflour

1 egg yolk

250 ml (8 fl oz) double
   cream

grated rind of 1 lemon

30 ml (2 tbsp) lemon juice

45 ml (3 tbsp) roughly
   chopped chervil

TO GARNISH

chervil sprigs

PREPARATION TIME
20 minutes
COOKING TIME
About 20 minutes
FREEZING
Not suitable

500 CALS PER SERVING

1. First make the sauce. Blend the cornflour with a little water in a small saucepan until smooth. Stir in the egg yolk, cream, lemon rind and juice, chervil, and pepper to taste. Set aside.

2. For the parcels, first remove the skin from the salmon if using fillets and halve each fillet lengthways. Trim and thinly slice the fennel. Melt 15 g ($\frac{1}{2}$ oz) of the butter in a frying pan. Add the fennel and fry gently for 3 minutes to soften. Cool slightly.

3. Preheat the oven to 200°C (400°F) Mark 6. Cut out six 25 cm (10 inch) circles of greaseproof paper. Spread each circle to within 2.5 cm (1 inch) of the edge with the remaining butter. Position a piece of salmon to one side of each circle.

4. Arrange a little fennel on each salmon fillet. Pare strips of lemon rind with a zester and scatter over the fish with the capers, chervil and seasoning.

5. Fold the paper over the filling and twist the edges together to seal completely. Place on a large baking sheet and bake for 20 minutes.

6. Slit one parcel open in the centre to test whether the salmon is cooked,

returning the parcels to the oven for a little longer if necessary.

7. Gently heat the sauce until slightly thickened. Split the top of each parcel open with a knife and garnish with sprigs of chervil. Serve with the chervil sauce.

NOTE: Test one parcel to see whether the salmon is cooked before slitting them all open. Pierce the thickest part of the salmon with a knife; if cooked, the flesh should have turned opaque.

VARIATION

Other small fish fillets or steaks, such as cod and haddock, can be cooked in the same way.

TECHNIQUE

Fold the paper over the fish to enclose. Twist the edges together to seal.

COD IN CRISP BATTER WITH LEMON AND PARSLEY SAUCE

There is nothing quite like crispy battered fresh white fish, served with a generous portion of chips. The homemade version is invariably far better than anything you buy from the local fish and chip shop. A creamy, yet tangy lemon and parsley sauce is the ideal accompaniment.

SERVES 4

700 g (1½ lb) cod or
   haddock fillet
30 ml (2 tbsp) plain flour
salt and pepper
oil for deep-frying
BATTER
200 g (7 oz) self-raising flour
2.5 ml (½ tsp) baking
   powder
2.5 ml (½ tsp) salt
SAUCE
25 g (1 oz) butter
15 ml (1 tbsp) plain flour
250 ml (8 fl oz) milk
60 ml (4 tbsp) chopped fresh
   parsley
finely grated rind of 1 lemon
juice of ½ lemon
45 ml (3 tbsp) double cream
TO GARNISH
lemon wedges

PREPARATION TIME
15 minutes, plus standing
COOKING TIME
About 15 minutes
FREEZING
Not suitable

655 CALS PER SERVING

1. First make the batter. Sift the flour, baking powder and salt into a bowl. Gradually whisk in 300 ml (½ pint) water to make a smooth batter. Leave to stand for 30 minutes to 1 hour.

2. Skin the fish if necessary and remove any small bones. Cut the fillets into slightly smaller pieces. Season the flour with salt and pepper and use to coat the fish pieces evenly.

3. To make the sauce, melt the butter in a small saucepan. Add the flour and cook, stirring, for 1 minute. Remove from the heat and gradually blend in the milk. Return to the heat and cook gently, stirring, until thickened. Stir in the parsley, lemon rind and juice, cream and seasoning.

4. Half fill a large deep saucepan or deep-fat fryer with oil and heat to 190°C (375°F). Cook the fish pieces in three batches. Coat them in the batter, lower into the oil and deep-fry for about 5 minutes until golden and crisp.

5. Lift the fish out with a slotted spoon and drain on kitchen paper. Keep warm while frying the remainder.

6. Meanwhile, gently reheat the sauce. Place the fish on warmed serving plates and garnish with lemon wedges. Serve with the lemon and parsley sauce, and vegetables of your choice.

NOTE: It's worth making chips to serve with the fish while you're using the deep fryer. Peel and cut the potatoes into chips. Put into the frying basket and lower into the oil. Deep-fry at 200°C (400°F) for 6-7 minutes until starting to colour. Lift the basket and drain the chips, then deep-fry for a further 3 minutes until golden and crisp. Drain, season and keep warm, while frying the fish.

TECHNIQUE

Carefully lower the pieces of battered fish into the oil and fry until golden.

SEAFOOD PIE WITH LEEKS AND BLUE CHEESE

Chunks of freshly poached cod, mixed with sautéed leeks and succulent prawns, under a blanket of creamy blue cheese sauce and a crisp potato topping, makes a superb pie to satisfy the largest appetite. This is a recipe to experiment with – using different types of fish, vegetables and cheese – but keep the quantities in the proportions given here for best results.

SERVES 4

700 g (1½ lb) floury
   potatoes
salt and pepper
450 g (1 lb) cod, haddock or
   whiting fillet
350 ml (12 fl oz) milk
350 g (12 oz) leeks
25 g (1 oz) butter
freshly grated nutmeg
225 g (8 oz) large peeled
   prawns
SAUCE
50 g (2 oz) butter
45 ml (3 tbsp) plain white
   flour
125 g (4 oz) blue Stilton
   cheese
60 ml (4 tbsp) single cream

PREPARATION TIME
40 minutes
COOKING TIME
About 45 minutes
FREEZING
Suitable: See note

675 CALS PER SERVING

1. Peel the potatoes and cut into 5 mm (¼ inch) thick slices. Bring a saucepan of salted water to the boil. Add the potatoes and cook for 5 minutes until partially softened. Drain.

2. Place the fish in a shallow pan. Pour on 50 ml (2 fl oz) of the milk. Season lightly, cover and poach for about 5 minutes until the fish flakes easily. Drain the fish, reserving the juices. Flake the fish, discarding the skin and any bones.

3. Trim and slice the leeks. Melt the butter in a pan and fry the leeks for 3 minutes, adding plenty of grated nutmeg. Lightly butter the sides of a 1.7 litre (3 pint) pie dish. Preheat the oven to 190°C (375°F) Mark 5.

4. To make the sauce, melt the butter in a small saucepan. Add the flour and cook, stirring, for 1 minute. Remove from the heat and gradually blend in the milk and the reserved fish poaching juices.

5. Return to the heat and cook, stirring, until thickened. Crumble in the cheese, then add the cream and seasoning.

6. Mix together the white fish, prawns and leeks in the prepared dish. Spoon over half of the cheese sauce. Layer the potatoes over the filling, then pour the remaining sauce over the potatoes. Place on a baking sheet and bake for about 45 minutes until bubbling and turning golden. Serve hot, with a green vegetable.

NOTE: The pie can be frozen once assembled but before baking, provided the prawns used have not been previously frozen.

TECHNIQUE

Mix together the white fish, prawns and sautéed leeks in the base of the dish.

ROAST LAMB WITH GARLIC AND MUSHROOM STUFFING

As with most great British roasts, lamb is traditionally cooked with little embellishment, to allow the flavour of the meat to dominate. To impart extra flavour, a robust garlic, mushroom and leek stuffing is included here. To save yourself time order a boned leg of lamb from the butcher several days in advance and use the bone to make the stock for the gravy.

SERVES 8

225 g (8 oz) brown
  mushrooms
6 large cloves garlic
1 leek
60 ml (4 tbsp) olive oil
45 ml (3 tbsp) chopped fresh
  oregano
salt and pepper
2.3 kg (5 lb) boned leg of
  lamb
45-60 ml (3-4 tbsp)
  redcurrant jelly
10 ml (2 tsp) wine vinegar
150 ml (¼ pint) red wine
300 ml (½ pint) lamb stock
TO GARNISH
herb sprigs

PREPARATION TIME
20 minutes, plus cooling
COOKING TIME
2½-3 hours
FREEZING
Not suitable

560 CALS PER SERVING

1. Wipe the mushrooms and peel the garlic. Place both in a food processor and work briefly until finely chopped. Trim and chop the leek. Heat the oil in a frying pan. Add the mushrooms, garlic and leek and fry for about 10 minutes until the mushroom juices have evaporated and the mixture has the consistency of a thick paste. Stir in the oregano and season with salt and pepper. Leave to cool.

2. Preheat the oven to 180°C (350°F) Mark 4. Open out the lamb and pack the stuffing down the centre. Fold the meat over the stuffing to enclose and tie with string. Place the lamb, joined-side down, in a roasting tin.

3. Roast the lamb for 25 minutes per 450 g (1 lb) plus 25 minutes for medium; 30 minutes per 450 g (1 lb) plus 30 minutes for well done.

4. Melt the redcurrant jelly in a small saucepan with the wine vinegar. Thirty minutes before the end of the roasting time, brush the lamb with the redcurrant glaze. Repeat several times before the end of the cooking time.

5. Remove the lamb from the tin and transfer to a warmed serving platter. Keep warm. Drain off the fat from the pan and stir in the wine and stock. Bring to the boil and boil until slightly reduced. Strain the gravy, if preferred, into a warmed sauceboat.

6. Remove the string from the lamb. Surround with herbs and serve accompanied by the gravy, and vegetables of your choice.

VARIATION

Whole roasted garlic bulbs make an attractive and delicious garnish. Roast them in their skins around the meat in the roasting tin.

TECHNIQUE

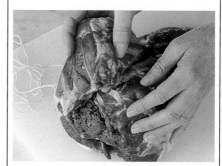

Spread the stuffing down the centre of the meat, then bring the meat over the stuffing and tie with string.

LAMB 'TOAD-IN-THE-HOLE' WITH CREAMY ONION SAUCE

Tender lamb cutlets encased in – and flavouring – a puffy, crisp batter, tastes even better than the more familiar sausage version. Just a hint of garlic and plenty of herbs bring out the flavour of the meat. The chunky onion sauce makes a lovely accompaniment, although a rich onion gravy would be equally good.

SERVES 4

8 lamb cutlets
2 cloves garlic, crushed
15 ml (1 tbsp) oil
BATTER
125 g (4 oz) plain flour
pinch of salt
2 eggs
300 ml (½ pint) milk
15 ml (1 tbsp) chopped fresh
   parsley
15 ml (1 tbsp) chopped fresh
   rosemary or thyme
SAUCE
1 large onion
25 g (1 oz) butter
15 ml (1 tbsp) plain flour
300 ml (½ pint) milk
2.5 ml (½ tsp) ground mace
1 bay leaf
2 tbsp (30 ml) double cream
salt and pepper
TO GARNISH
flat-leaved parsley
thyme sprigs

PREPARATION TIME
25 minutes
COOKING TIME
About 40 minutes
FREEZING
Not suitable

510 CALS PER SERVING

1. Preheat the oven to 220°C (425°F) Mark 7. Trim excess fat from the lamb cutlets, then spread with the garlic. Heat the oil in a frying pan and fry the lamb on both sides until sealed and browned.

2. Lightly grease the sides of a shallow 1.2 litre (2 pint) ovenproof dish. Lay the lamb cutlets in the dish, propping the thin ends up to raise them slightly.

3. To make the batter, sift the flour and salt into a bowl. Make a well in the centre and add the eggs with a little of the milk. Whisk together the eggs and remaining milk, gradually incorporating the flour to make a paste. Beat in the remaining milk and herbs.

4. Cook the lamb in the oven for 5 minutes, then pour the batter around the lamb and return to the oven. Reduce the temperature to 200°C (400°F) Mark 6 and cook for a further 35 minutes or until the batter is well risen and crisp.

5. Meanwhile make the sauce. Peel and finely chop the onion. Melt the butter in a saucepan and fry the onion for about 3 minutes until beginning to colour. Stir in the flour, then gradually blend in the milk. Add the mace and bay leaf and cook, stirring, for 1 minute until slightly thickened. Leave to simmer very gently

for 10 minutes until thickened. Remove the bay leaf and add the cream and seasoning.

6. Serve the lamb in batter piping hot, garnished with herbs and accompanied by the onion sauce.

NOTE: If you prefer lamb slightly pink, choose thick cutlets and omit the 5 minutes pre-baking. Instead, simply preheat the dish, with a little oil added.

VARIATIONS

● Use 450 g (1 lb) good quality sausages instead of the lamb.
● Replace the lamb with chunks of rump steak and kidney.

TECHNIQUE

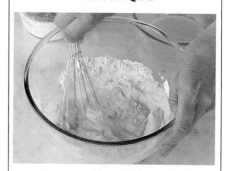

For the batter, whisk together the eggs and a little of the milk, gradually incorporating the flour to make a paste.

PORK WITH PEASE PUDDING

Another sturdy survivor of traditional British fare, this delicious 'one-pot' dish is exceptionally easy to make, provided you have a very large pan, and remember to order the salt pork from the butcher several days in advance. If you haven't the time to order, a piece of gammon is a good option. Alternatively you could use fresh pork, but this won't have quite the same intensity of flavour. Pease pudding is traditionally thick enough to slice like a cake, but here it is creamy smooth, drizzled with oil and grilled to colour.

SERVES 6

1.8 kg (4 lb) piece salt pork
   or gammon
225 g (8 oz) baby onions
350 g (12 oz) small carrots
350 g (12 oz) baby turnips
2 celery sticks
2 bay leaves
salt and pepper
PEASE PUDDING
225 g (8 oz) split yellow peas
10 ml (2 tsp) chopped fresh
   thyme
10 ml (2 tsp) chopped fresh
   mint
5 ml (1 tsp) caster sugar
25 g (1 oz) butter
1 egg yolk
a little olive oil
extra herbs, for sprinkling

PREPARATION TIME
30 minutes, plus soaking
COOKING TIME
About 1¾ hours
FREEZING
Not suitable

590 CALS PER SERVING

1. For the pease pudding, place the split peas in a bowl, cover with plenty of cold water and leave to soak overnight.

2. Drain the peas and turn onto a pudding cloth or large square of muslin. Sprinkle with the herbs, sugar and seasoning, then bring the edges of the cloth up over the peas and secure with string, allowing plenty of room for the peas to expand.

3. Place the meat in a large pan and cover with water. Bring to the boil and skim off any scum using a slotted spoon. Add the pudding bag to the pan, securing the string to the pan handle.

4. Peel the onions, carrots and turnips; leave whole. Roughly chop the celery. Put the vegetables in the pan around the meat, with the bay leaves and seasoning. Simmer gently, allowing 25 minutes per 450 g (1 lb) pork.

5. Preheat the grill to medium. Remove the pease pudding bag from the pan and drain thoroughly. Tip into a bowl and mash well, beating in the butter and egg yolk. When light and fluffy, place spoonfuls onto a lightly greased baking sheet. Drizzle with oil, seasoning and extra chopped herbs, and grill until coloured.

6. Lift the meat out of the pan and carve into slices. Drain the vegetables, reserving the cooking liquor. Arrange the meat on warmed serving plates with the pease pudding and vegetables. Serve the cooking liquor as gravy.

NOTE: If you prefer less soft vegetables, add to the pan about 30 minutes from the end of the cooking time.

VARIATION

Green split peas or red lentils can be used instead of the yellow split peas.

TECHNIQUE

Bring the edges of the cloth up over the peas and secure with string.

STEAK AND KIDNEY PUDDING

Of all British favourites, this dish seems to win the greatest acclaim as we remember the inviting aroma and rich meaty gravy seeping into the suety pastry case. Fresh oysters, once the food of the poor, were frequently used to stretch the meat. Here a few canned oysters are included instead to impart a delicious smoky flavour.

SERVES 6

FILLING

700 g (1½ lb) braising or
 stewing steak
225 g (8 oz) ox kidney
60 ml (4 tbsp) plain flour
salt and pepper
2 small onions
45 ml (3 tbsp) oil
450 ml (¾ pint) beef stock
90 ml (6 tbsp) port
225 g (8 oz) mushrooms
8 canned smoked oysters
 (optional)
PASTRY
300 g (10 oz) self-raising
 flour
2.5 ml (½ tsp) salt
150 g (5 oz) suet

PREPARATION TIME
35 minutes
COOKING TIME
About 3½ hours
FREEZING
Not suitable

540 CALS PER SERVING

1. Trim the meat and cut into 2 cm (¾ inch) pieces. Remove the white core from the kidney, then cut into 1 cm (½ inch) chunks. Season the flour with salt and pepper and use to coat the meat.

2. Peel and chop the onions. Heat the oil in a large frying pan and fry the steak in batches until browned on all sides. Transfer to a flameproof casserole or heavy-based saucepan, using a slotted spoon. Brown the kidney in the oil remaining in the frying pan, then transfer to the casserole. Add the onion to the frying pan and fry gently for about 10 minutes until soft, adding a little extra oil if necessary. Add to the meat with the stock, port and seasoning. Bring to the boil, reduce the heat, cover and simmer gently for 1¼ hours.

3. To make the pastry, sift the flour and salt into a bowl and stir in the suet. Add 175 ml (6 fl oz) cold water and mix to a soft dough using a round-bladed knife, adding a little extra water if the pastry is dry.

4. Roll out a scant three quarters of the dough on a lightly floured surface. Use to line a 1.7 litre (3 pint) pudding basin.

5. Halve any large mushrooms and stir the mushrooms into the meat with the oysters if using. Turn into the lined basin.

Brush the top edge of the pastry with water. Roll out the remainder to make a lid and lay over the pudding, pressing the edges together to seal.

6. Cover the basin with a pleated, double thickness layer of greaseproof paper, securing under the rim with string. Cover with foil and place in a steamer or on an upturned saucer in a large saucepan. Pour in enough hot water to come halfway up the sides of the basin. Cover with a lid and steam for 2 hours, checking the water level occasionally.

7. Remove the foil and greaseproof paper and loosen the edges of the pudding. Invert onto a serving plate and serve at once, with vegetables in season.

TECHNIQUE

Use three quarters of the pastry to line the basin, lightly pressing onto the base and around the sides in an even layer.

BEEF AND BEER STEW WITH PARSNIP PURÉE

This wonderfully dark, glossy stew is enriched with good strong beer and a hint of treacle. A creamy parsnip purée is the perfect robust accompaniment to soak up the delicious flavoursome juices. Serve with roasted parsnips too if you like, and sautéed cabbage or another green vegetable.

SERVES 6

1.1 kg (2½ lb) chuck or
  blade beef
30 ml (2 tbsp) plain flour
salt and pepper
3 large onions
4 celery sticks
several thyme sprigs
2 bay leaves
450 g (1 lb) turnips
25 g (1 oz) beef dripping or
  lard
450 ml (¾ pint) beef stock
450 ml (¾ pint) strong beer
45 ml (3 tbsp) black treacle
PARSNIP PUREÉ
900 g (2 lb) parsnips
45 ml (3 tbsp) double cream
TO GARNISH
celery leaves

PREPARATION TIME
25 minutes
COOKING TIME
About 1¾ hours
FREEZING
Suitable: Except parsnip purée

500 CALS PER SERVING

1. Cut the meat into large chunks, discarding excess fat. Season the flour with salt and pepper and use to coat the meat. Peel and thinly slice the onions. Cut two 5 cm (2 inch) lengths of celery. Tie in bundles with the thyme and bay leaves. Cut the remaining celery into chunks. Peel the turnips and cut into large chunks.

2. Preheat the oven to 160°C (325°F) Mark 3. Heat the dripping or lard in a large flameproof casserole. Add half of the meat and fry, turning, until lightly browned. Remove with a slotted spoon and fry the remainder; remove.

3. Add the onions and celery to the pan and fry gently until softened. Return the meat to the pan and add the herb bundles. Stir in the stock, beer and treacle, then add the turnips. Bring just to the boil, reduce the heat, cover with a lid and transfer to the oven. Cook for 1½ hours or until the meat and vegetables are tender.

4. Peel the parsnips and cut into 7.5 cm (3 inch) lengths; cut lengthways into even-sized pieces. Put the parsnips into a saucepan and cover with water. Bring to the boil, lower the heat and simmer for about 15 minutes until completely tender.

5. Drain the parsnips thoroughly and return to the pan. Add the cream and seasoning and mash well until completely smooth.

6. Divide the stew between warmed serving plates and add spoonfuls of the parsnip purée. Garnish with celery leaves to serve.

VARIATION

Use Guinness instead of the beer.

TECHNIQUE

Tie the celery pieces and herbs into small bundles with cotton string.

CALVES LIVER WITH BLACK PUDDING AND BACON

This is a deliciously simple recipe that's perfect for an easy supper. Tender calves liver is flash-fried with black pudding and bacon, and served with a quick sauce – made by enriching the pan juices with cream and cider. Tangy dessert apples are wrapped in the bacon to add a refreshing contrast.

SERVES 4

4 slices smoked streaky
  bacon, derinded
1 dessert apple
700 g (1½ lb) calves liver
125 g (4 oz) black pudding
15 ml (1 tbsp) oil
25 g (1 oz) butter
150 ml (¼ pint) double
  cream
125 ml (4 fl oz) medium
  cider
20 ml (4 tsp) chopped fresh
  sage
salt and pepper
TO GARNISH
sage and parsley sprigs

PREPARATION TIME
15 minutes
COOKING TIME
8 minutes
FREEZING
Not suitable

695 CALS PER SERVING

1. Stretch each bacon rasher with the back of a knife, then cut in half to give 8 strips. Cut the apple into 8 wedges, cutting away the core.

2. Trim the liver and cut into slightly smaller pieces. Slice the black pudding. Heat the oil with the butter in a large frying pan. Add the apple wedges and fry gently for 2 minutes. Remove with a slotted spoon.

3. Wrap an apple wedge in each bacon strip and secure with a wooden cocktail stick. Return to the pan and fry over a moderate heat for 2 minutes, turning frequently. Add the black pudding and cook for 1 minute on each side.

4. Remove the bacon rolls and black pudding from the pan with a slotted spoon and keep warm. Add the calves liver to the pan and cook for 30 seconds on each side. Drain.

5. Add the cream, cider, sage and seasoning to the pan. Bring to the boil and return the liver to the pan. Lower the heat and simmer for 1 minute to heat through. Arrange the liver, bacon rolls and black pudding on warmed serving plates and pour over the sauce. Serve at once, garnished with sage and parsley.

NOTE: Calves liver has a wonderful flavour and texture, which are easily spoiled by overcooking, so do take care. The liver is cooked as soon as it's seared and golden brown.

VARIATION

Omit the black pudding and use quartered lamb's kidney instead.

TECHNIQUE

Quickly fry the liver for about 30 seconds. Turn over with a fish slice and cook for a further 30 seconds.

VENISON CASSEROLE WITH RED WINE AND SPICES

Venison has recently regained popularity, and exceptionally lean steaks are widely stocked in supermarkets throughout the winter. These are ideal for marinating in wine with spices, and then casseroling to a moist tenderness. Rather rich in flavour, venison is best lightened with plenty of vegetables. Creamed potatoes and shredded, sautéed cabbage are suitable accompaniments.

SERVES 6-8

900 g (2 lb) lean venison

1 large onion

2 carrots

3 garlic cloves, peeled

2 bay leaves

4-6 whole cloves

15 ml (1 tbsp) allspice

60 ml (4 tbsp) brandy

300 ml (½ pint) red wine

225 g (8 oz) baby onions

½ small celeriac

125 g (4 oz) rindless streaky bacon

30 ml (2 tbsp) plain flour

salt and pepper

30 ml (2 tbsp) oil

300 ml (½ pint) beef stock

1 cinnamon stick, halved

225 g (8 oz) wild mushrooms

15 ml (1 tbsp) wine vinegar

15 ml (1 tbsp) redcurrant jelly

TO GARNISH

bay leaves

PREPARATION TIME
45 minutes, plus 2-3 days marinating
COOKING TIME
About 2 hours
FREEZING Suitable

420-315 CALS PER SERVING

1. Cut the venison into chunks and place in a large bowl. Peel and quarter the onion. Peel and roughly chop the carrots. Add the vegetables to the bowl with the garlic, bay leaves, cloves, allspice, brandy and wine. Cover and leave to marinate in the refrigerator for 2-3 days, turning daily.

2. Preheat the oven to 160°C (325°F) Mark 3. Peel the baby onions and leave whole. Peel the celeriac and cut into chunks. Dice the bacon. Thoroughly drain the venison and pat dry on kitchen paper, reserving the marinade. Season the flour with salt and pepper and use to coat the meat.

3. Heat the oil in a flameproof casserole. Add the venison and sear on all sides. Remove with a slotted spoon. Add the onions and bacon to the casserole and fry for 3 minutes. Return the venison to the casserole with the celeriac. Strain the marinade juices over the meat, then add the stock and cinnamon stick.

4. Bring just to the boil, reduce the heat and cover with a tight-fitting lid. Cook in the oven for 1 hour. Add the mushrooms, wine vinegar and redcurrant jelly to the casserole and return to the oven for a further 1 hour.

5. Ladle the stew onto warmed serving plates and garnish with bay leaves.

NOTE: This is a good stew for cooking a day in advance and reheating, as it helps to further tenderise the meat.

VARIATION

If wild mushrooms are unobtainable use either chestnut mushrooms or flat mushrooms instead.

TECHNIQUE

Marinate the venison chunks in the brandy and wine, with the vegetables, herbs and spices.

PHEASANT WITH SMOKED BACON AND MUSHROOMS

This recipe 'roasts' pheasant with the addition of wine and stock to keep this naturally dry-textured bird as moist and succulent as possible. Richly flavoured dried mushrooms, garlic, juniper berries and smoked bacon add plenty of flavour to the juices.

SERVES 4

15 g (½ oz) dried porcini or mixed dried mushrooms

1 small onion

125 g (4 oz) smoked bacon, in one piece

10 juniper berries

2 garlic cloves, crushed

2 oven-ready pheasants

25 g (1 oz) butter

10 ml (2 tsp) plain white flour

300 ml (½ pint) red wine

150 ml (¼ pint) chicken or pheasant stock (see note)

175 g (6 oz) chestnut or brown mushrooms

30 ml (2 tbsp) redcurrant jelly

TO GARNISH

125 g (4 oz) puff pastry

15 ml (1 tbsp) finely chopped fresh rosemary

beaten egg yolk, to glaze

flat-leaved parsley

PREPARATION TIME
35 minutes
COOKING TIME
About 1 hour
FREEZING
Not suitable

420 CALS PER SERVING

1. Rinse the dried mushrooms twice and place in a bowl with 300 ml (½ pint) warm water. Let soak for 20 minutes.

2. Preheat the oven to 220°C (425°F) Mark 7. For the garnish, roll out the pastry to about a 5 mm (¼ inch) thickness. Scatter with the rosemary, then roll out further to about a 3 mm (⅛ inch) thickness. Cut out small triangular shapes and transfer to a dampened baking sheet. Brush with beaten egg yolk and bake for about 8 minutes until puffed and golden; set aside. Lower the oven temperature to 200°C (400°F) Mark 6.

3. Meanwhile, peel and finely chop the onion. Dice the bacon. Lightly crush the juniper berries.

4. Spread the garlic over the pheasants. Melt the butter in a frying pan and sear the pheasants on all sides. Transfer to a large casserole dish with the juniper.

5. Add the onion and bacon to the frying pan and fry gently for 10 minutes. Stir in the flour, add the wine and stock and bring to the boil. Pour over the pheasants, cover and bake for 25 minutes.

6. Drain and rinse the dried mushrooms; halve the fresh mushrooms. Tuck both around the pheasants in the casserole. Return to the oven and cook, uncovered, for a further 20-25 minutes. Test the pheasant by piercing the thickest part of the thigh with a skewer; the juices should run clear.

7. Transfer the pheasants and mushrooms to a serving plate, using a slotted spoon; keep warm. Add the redcurrant jelly to the cooking juices and heat until the jelly dissolves. Pour a little over the pheasants and serve the rest in a sauceboat. Serve the pheasant and mushrooms garnished with the pastries and parsley, and accompanied by the sauce.

NOTE: If available, use pheasant giblets to make the stock. Simmer in sufficient water to cover with an onion, a carrot, herbs and seasoning for 1 hour; strain.

TECHNIQUE

Fry the pheasants in a large pan, turning carefully until seared on all sides.

ROAST CHICKEN WITH A DEVILLED SAUCE

When roasts were the mainstay of British cooking, 'devilling' with a hot sauce was a popular way of reviving interest in leftovers. Here, the idea is put to better use: a hot, tangy base is used for glazing a large chicken during roasting; it also forms the basis of a delicious sauce. Accompany with a crisp salad and new potatoes.

SERVES 6

2.3 kg (5 lb) large chicken
3 garlic cloves
1 large onion
DEVILLED SAUCE
30 ml (2 tbsp) mango or
    sweet fruit chutney
25 g (1 oz) butter
30 ml (2 tbsp)
    Worcestershire sauce
30 ml (2 tbsp) grainy English
    mustard
5 ml (1 tsp) paprika
45 ml (3 tbsp) freshly
    squeezed orange juice
salt and pepper
450 g (1 lb) tomatoes
TO SERVE
90 ml (3 fl oz) crème fraîche
leafy herbs (eg basil, lovage
    or lemon balm), to
    garnish

PREPARATION TIME
20 minutes
COOKING TIME
About 1¾ hours
FREEZING
Not suitable

270 CALS PER SERVING

1. Preheat the oven to 190°C (375°F) Mark 5. To make the devilled sauce, chop any large pieces in the chutney. Melt the butter. Mix together the butter, chutney, Worcestershire sauce, mustard, paprika, orange juice and seasoning.

2. Peel and chop the garlic and onion; place in the cavity of the chicken, then place the chicken in a roasting tin. Baste the skin all over with the devilled sauce. Roast in the oven, basting frequently with the sauce for 1¾ hours, or until the juices run clear when the thickest part of the thigh is pierced with a skewer. At the end of the cooking time the chicken should be slightly charred, but cover with foil towards the end of cooking if it becomes over-blackened.

3. In the meantime, place the tomatoes in a bowl and cover with boiling water. Leave for 1 minute, then drain and peel away the skins. Scoop out the seeds, then roughly chop the tomatoes; set aside.

4. Transfer the chicken to a warmed serving platter and keep warm. Skim off the fat from the juices in the roasting tin, then stir in the tomatoes and any remaining devilled sauce. Transfer the sauce to a food processor or blender and process briefly until the mixture is pulpy but retaining a little texture.

Return to the pan and heat through, seasoning with salt and pepper to taste.

5. Meanwhile warm the crème fraîche in a small saucepan.

6. Garnish the chicken with plenty of herbs and serve with the devilled sauce and crème fraîche.

VARIATION

For a more fiery sauce, add a finely chopped chilli to the devilled mixture before basting.

TECHNIQUE

Use the devilled mixture to generously baste the chicken during cooking.

TURKEY AND HAM PIE WITH CHESTNUTS

This festive pie works well with ready-diced packs of turkey from the supermarket. It is also an excellent way of using up Christmas leftovers. The flavourful juices are laced with cream, and cranberries are added for a piquant contrast. All are encased under a deliciously crumbly potato pastry crust.

SERVES 8-10

450 g (1 lb) turkey breast
450 g (1 lb) boneless turkey thigh
45 ml (3 tbsp) plain flour
salt and pepper
350 g (12 oz) cooked ham
2 large onions
50 g (2 oz) butter
750 ml (1¼ pints) chicken stock
freshly grated nutmeg
350 g (12 oz) vacuum-packed chestnuts
15 ml (1 tbsp) chopped fresh thyme
150 g (5 oz) fresh or frozen cranberries
150 ml (¼ pint) double cream
PASTRY
1 large potato
450 g (1 lb) plain white flour
125 g (4 oz) butter
150 g (5 oz) lard
TO FINISH
beaten egg, to glaze
coarse salt, for sprinkling

PREPARATION TIME
50 minutes, plus cooling
COOKING TIME About 1¼ hours
FREEZING Suitable

945-755 CALS PER SERVING

1. Dice the turkey meat. Season the flour with salt and pepper and use to coat the meat. Dice the ham. Peel and chop the onions.

2. Melt the butter in a large frying pan. Add half of the turkey and fry quickly on all sides until golden. Remove with a slotted spoon and set aside; fry the rest of the turkey; remove. Add the onions to the fat remaining in the pan and cook gently for about 10 minutes, until soft.

3. Stir in the stock, plenty of nutmeg and seasoning; cook, stirring, until thickened. Combine the turkey, ham, chestnuts and thyme in a flameproof casserole and pour on the stock mixture. Cover and cook very gently for 30 minutes. Stir in the cranberries and cream.

4. Transfer the turkey and ham mixture to a 2 litre (3½ pint) large shallow pie dish. Place a pie funnel in the centre and add enough of the cooking juices to half fill the dish. Leave to cool.

5. Meanwhile make the pastry. Peel and dice the potato, and cook in boiling salted water until tender. Drain well and mash. Sift the flour into a bowl. Add the fats, cut into small pieces, and rub in using fingertips. Add the potato and mix with a round-bladed knife, adding a little

cold water to make a smooth, firm dough. Wrap in cling film and chill in the refrigerator for 30 minutes.

6. Preheat the oven to 200°C (400°F) Mark 6. Roll out the pastry and use to cover the pie. Make a hole in the centre and decorate with shapes cut from the pastry trimmings if liked. Brush with beaten egg to glaze and scatter with a little coarse salt. Bake for 40 minutes until crisp and golden. Serve hot, with seasonal vegetables and any reserved cooking juices in a sauceboat.

NOTE: Vacuum-packed chestnuts make a great substitute for fresh ones. Dried chestnuts are also suitable, but remember to soak them overnight before using.

TECHNIQUE

For the pastry, stir the mashed potato into the rubbed-in mixture using a round-bladed knife.

SPICED RAISIN PUDDINGS WITH DEMERARA LEMON BUTTER

Few of us with a passion for food can resist the temptation of a hot, steaming 'British' pudding. There are many wonderful versions, but this light-as-air spicy sponge – specked with raisins and stem ginger – is one of the best. A sweet, syrupy lemon-flavoured butter is the perfect complement.

SERVES 8

1 piece preserved stem
   ginger in syrup, about 15 g
   ($\frac{1}{2}$ oz)
175 g (6 oz) unsalted butter,
   softened
175 g (6 oz) caster sugar
3 eggs, lightly beaten
225 g (8 oz) self-raising flour
7.5 ml (1$\frac{1}{2}$ tsp) baking
   powder
5 ml (1 tsp) ground mixed
   spice
2.5 ml ($\frac{1}{2}$ tsp) ground
   cinnamon
75 g (3 oz) raisins
a little milk
SAUCE
75 g (3 oz) unsalted butter
175 g (6 oz) demerara sugar
grated rind and juice of
   2 small lemons

PREPARATION TIME
25 minutes
COOKING TIME
40-45 minutes
FREEZING
Suitable: See note

560 CALS PER SERVING

1. Preheat the oven to 180°C (350°F) Mark 4. Grease the bases and sides of 8 individual 185 ml (6 fl oz) metal pudding basins. Chop the ginger into tiny pieces.

2. In a bowl, cream together the butter and sugar until pale and fluffy. Add the eggs, a little at a time, beating well after each addition, and adding a little of the flour to prevent curdling.

3. Sift the remaining flour, baking powder and spices over the bowl. Add the raisins and chopped ginger and gradually fold in, using a large metal spoon. Stir in sufficient milk to give a soft, dropping consistency.

4. Divide the mixture among the prepared tins and level the surfaces. Stand in a roasting tin and pour boiling water around the tins to a depth of 1 cm ($\frac{1}{2}$ inch). Cover the roasting tin with foil. Bake for 40-45 minutes until the sponges have risen and feel firm to the touch.

5. Meanwhile, make the sauce. Melt the butter in a small saucepan. Add the sugar and heat gently for 2-3 minutes until bubbling. Add the lemon rind and juice and cook gently to make a buttery syrup.

6. Loosen the edges of the puddings with a knife, then invert onto warmed serving plates. Pour a little sauce over each one and serve with cream or crème fraîche.

NOTE: The puddings can be frozen uncooked, for a later date. Bake as above, from frozen, allowing an extra 5 minutes cooking time.

VARIATIONS

● Use chopped dates, dried figs or prunes instead of raisins.
● Replace the lemon in the sauce with orange rind and juice.

TECHNIQUE

Stir sufficient milk into the mixture to give a soft dropping consistency.

APPLE BRAMBLE PUDDING

This excellent dessert, packed with soft fruits and sweet, juicy bread slices, bears a strong resemblance to a 'summer pudding'. Bramley apples, blackberries, and raspberries are lightly cooked in a syrupy butter, then layered with soft bread and baked to a golden crust. Serve with homemade creamy custard (see page 6), or cream if you are short of time.

SERVES 6

125 g (4 oz) unsalted butter
75 g (3 oz) demerara sugar
700 g (1½ lb) cooking apples
30 ml (2 tbsp) lemon juice
350 g (12 oz) blackberries
225 g (8 oz) raspberries
125 g (4 oz) red or
  blackcurrants
6 slices traditional white loaf
15 ml (1 tbsp) oil
a little demerara sugar, for
  sprinkling

PREPARATION TIME
25 minutes
COOKING TIME
25 minutes
FREEZING
Not suitable

430 CALS PER SERVING

1. Preheat the oven to 200°C (400°F) Mark 6. Lightly grease a 1.7 litre (3 pint) ovenproof dish. Melt 50 g (2 oz) of the butter in a large pan. Add the sugar and stir until beginning to dissolve.

2. Peel, core and thickly slice the apples and add to the pan. Cook gently, stirring frequently, for 5 minutes. Add the lemon juice, blackberries, raspberries and red or blackcurrants; toss lightly to combine.

3. Spoon half the fruit mixture into the base of the ovenproof dish. Remove the crusts from the bread if preferred. Melt the remaining butter in a frying pan with the oil, add half of the bread slices and fry until beginning to brown on the underside. Remove with a fish slice and lay the slices, browned sides uppermost, over the fruits in the dish. (Reserve the butter and oil).

4. Spread the rest of the fruits and juices over the bread. Cut the remaining bread into triangles and arrange over the fruit in the dish. Brush liberally with the reserved butter and oil, then sprinkle with the demerara sugar. Bake in the oven for about 25 minutes until the bread topping is deep golden. Serve with custard or cream.

VARIATIONS

Virtually any combination of soft fruits can be used in this pudding, but avoid too many blackcurrants as their flavour will dominate.

TECHNIQUE

Spoon the remaining fruit mixture over the fried bread slices, then cover with the bread triangles, packing down lightly.

TREACLE TART

This robust pudding illustrates how the simplest ingredients can be transformed into the most heavenly dessert. Here, breadcrumbs are mixed with plenty of golden syrup and lemon to cut the sweetness, then baked in a semi-sweet pastry case. Spoonfuls of slightly melting clotted cream ice cream (page 78) are the perfect indulgent accompaniment. Alternatively, serve with a dollop of crème fraîche.

SERVES 8-10

PASTRY
225 g (8 oz) plain white flour
150 g (5 oz) unsalted butter
1 egg yolk
15 g (½ oz) caster sugar
FILLING
700 g (1½ lb) golden syrup
175 g (6 oz) white
   breadcrumbs
grated rind of 3 lemons
2 eggs

PREPARATION TIME
25 minutes, plus chilling
COOKING TIME
25-50 minutes
FREEZING
Suitable

620 - 495 CALS PER SERVING

1. To make the pastry, sift the flour and put in a food processor. Add the butter, cut into small pieces, and work until the mixture resembles breadcrumbs. Add the egg yolk, sugar and about 30 ml (2 tbsp) cold water; process briefly to a firm dough. Turn onto a lightly floured surface and knead lightly, then wrap in cling film and chill in the refrigerator for 30 minutes.

2. Preheat the oven to 180°C (350°F) Mark 4. Roll out the pastry on a lightly floured surface and use to line a 25 cm (10 inch) shallow fluted flan tin, about 4 cm (1½ inches) deep. Trim off the excess pastry and flute the edges. Prick the base with a fork.

3. For the filling, lightly heat the golden syrup in a saucepan until thinned in consistency. Remove from the heat and mix with the breadcrumbs and lemon rind. Lightly beat the eggs and stir into the syrup mixture. Pour the filling into the pastry case.

4. Bake in the oven for about 45-50 minutes until the filling is lightly set and turning golden. Allow to cool slightly. Serve warm, with ice cream or crème fraîche.

TECHNIQUE

Pour the prepared syrup filling into the pastry case.

RATAFIA BAKEWELL TART

This recipe revives one of our most famous puddings to its original glory, a far cry from the bland, shop bought imitations. Here, a deep almondy sponge and thick apricot conserve are enclosed in a deep-sided pastry case and topped with caramel oranges. Served warm or cold, with dollops of cream or crème fraîche, the tart is equally good with or without the caramel orange topping.

SERVES 8

PASTRY
225 g (8 oz) plain white flour
50 g (2 oz) lightly salted butter
50 g (2 oz) white vegetable fat
FILLING
60 ml (4 tbsp) apricot conserve or jam
50 g (2 oz) ratafia biscuits
75 g (3 oz) unsalted butter
3 eggs
125 g (4 oz) caster sugar
5 ml (1 tsp) almond essence
125 g (4 oz) ground almonds
TO SERVE
caramel oranges (optional)
icing sugar, for dusting

PREPARATION TIME
30 minutes, plus chilling
COOKING TIME
About 50 minutes
FREEZING
Suitable: Without topping

500 CALS PER SERVING

1. To make the pastry, sift the flour into a bowl. Add the fats, cut into small pieces, and rub in with the fingertips. Stir in enough water to make a firm dough. Knead lightly, then wrap in cling film and chill for 30 minutes.

2. Preheat the oven to 200°C (400°F) Mark 6. Preheat a baking sheet. Roll out the pastry on a lightly floured surface and use to line a 23 cm (9 inch) spring-release cake tin. Spread the apricot conserve over the base. Halve the ratafia biscuits.

3. Melt the butter; set aside. Place the eggs and sugar in a large bowl and whisk until the mixture is thick enough for the whisk to leave a trail when lifted from the bowl. Pour in the melted butter, around the edge of the bowl. Add the almond essence and scatter over the ground almonds and ratafia biscuits. Fold in carefully, using a large metal spoon, until just combined.

4. Turn the mixture into the pastry-lined tin. Place on the preheated baking sheet and bake for 10 minutes. Reduce the oven temperature to 180°C (350°F) Mark 4 and bake for a further 40 minutes or until the filling is firm and set.

5. If serving caramel oranges, arrange some on top of the tart, spooning a little of the syrup over them. Allow the tart to cool slightly, then remove from tin and place on a serving plate. Dust edges with icing sugar and serve warm or cold. Accompany with cream or crème fraîche, and the rest of the oranges if serving.

NOTE: Don't worry if the tart sinks slightly in the centre. This accentuates its lovely cracked crust.

CARAMEL ORANGES
Pare strips of rind from 1 orange. Peel 3 oranges, discarding all white pith, then slice thinly. Dissolve 175 g (6 oz) sugar in 600 ml (1 pint) water in a heavy-based pan over a low heat. Increase heat and boil steadily for 5 minutes. Add the orange slices and rind strips. Bring to the boil, then simmer gently for 15 minutes. Remove the fruit and rind with a slotted spoon and cook the syrup for a further 20 minutes until pale golden. Return fruit to syrup.

TECHNIQUE

Carefully fold the ground almonds and ratafia biscuits into the whisked mixture until just combined.

CINNAMON BREAD WITH STRAWBERRY COMPOTE

Steeping chunks of bread in sweetened milk, then frying it to a crisp case has long been a thrifty way of revitalising stale bread. This recipe enhances the idea, tossing the bread in spiced sugar and serving it with lightly poached strawberries. Served with whipped cream, the flavour combination is really delicious.

SERVES 6

STRAWBERRY COMPOTE
450 g (1 lb) strawberries
25 g (1 oz) caster sugar
1 cinnamon stick, halved
45 ml (3 tbsp) redcurrant
   jelly
squeeze of lemon juice, to
   taste
CINNAMON BREAD
6 thick slices white bread,
   about 2 cm (¾ inch) thick
   (see note)
3 egg yolks
2.5 ml (½ tsp) vanilla
   essence
65 g (2½ oz) caster sugar
150 ml (¼ pint) double
   cream
50 ml (2 fl oz) milk
50 g (2 oz) unsalted butter
15 ml (1 tbsp) oil
1.25 ml (¼ tsp) ground
   cinnamon
TO DECORATE
lemon balm or mint sprigs

PREPARATION TIME
20 minutes, plus soaking
COOKING TIME
About 10 minutes
FREEZING Not suitable

430 CALS PER SERVING

1. To make the compote, hull the strawberries and halve any large ones. Place in a saucepan with the sugar and cinnamon stick. Cover and heat very gently until the strawberries are beginning to soften.

2. Melt the redcurrant jelly in a separate saucepan with 15 ml (1 tbsp) water. Pour over the strawberries. Stir lightly and remove from the heat. Add a little lemon juice to taste.

3. Cut a 7.5 cm (3 inch) square from each bread slice. Cut each square in half diagonally to make triangles. Lightly beat the egg yolks with the vanilla essence, 15 ml (1 tbsp) sugar, the cream and milk.

4. Place the bread slices in a single layer on two large plates. Pour the egg mixture over them and leave to stand for 10 minutes until absorbed.

5. Melt the butter with the oil in a large frying pan. Add half the bread triangles and fry for 2 minutes or until golden on the undersides. Turn the bread and fry for another 1 minute. Drain and keep warm while frying the remainder, adding a little more butter to the pan if necessary.

6. Mix the remaining sugar and cinnamon together and use to coat the fried bread. Arrange on serving plates with the strawberries and juice. Decorate with lemon balm or mint sprigs and serve with cream or crème fraîche.

NOTE: Use bread that's one or two days old if available, as it will be easier to cut and soak.

VARIATIONS

Use raspberries instead of the strawberries, heating them briefly in the melted redcurrant jelly, rather than softening them first. Lightly poached sweet plums or apricots would also work well.

TECHNIQUE

Once the bread is golden on the underside, flip over with a large palette knife and fry for a further minute.

ROSE BAVAROIS WITH SOFT FRUITS

Creamy, light-as-air and gently flavoured with rosewater, this delicate mousse makes a perfect finale to a summer's meal. The smooth texture of the bavarois is beautifully balanced by the sweetness of the fruits. Serve in a large dish or in tall stemmed glasses. Delicate dessert biscuits make a lovely accompaniment.

SERVES 10-12

20 ml (4 tsp) powdered
  gelatine
6 egg yolks
125 g (4 oz) caster sugar
15 ml (1 tbsp) cornflour
600 ml (1 pint) milk
450 ml (¾ pint) single cream
10 red rose petals
15-30 ml (1-2 tbsp)
  rosewater
300 ml (½ pint) double
  cream

TO FINISH

350 g (12 oz) raspberries
75 g (3 oz) blueberries
60 ml (4 tbsp) redcurrant
  jelly
sugared rose petals, to
  decorate (see right)

PREPARATION TIME
35 minutes, plus chilling
COOKING TIME
7 minutes
FREEZING
Not suitable

385-320 CALS PER SERVING

1. Sprinkle the gelatine over 45 ml (3 tbsp) water in a small bowl and leave to soften. In a bowl, beat the egg yolks with the sugar, cornflour and a little of the milk. Place the remaining milk in a saucepan with the single cream and bring almost to the boil.

2. Pour the hot creamy milk over the egg yolk mixture, whisking constantly, then return to the saucepan. Cook gently, stirring all the time, until thickened enough to thinly coat the back of the spoon; do not boil or the custard will curdle.

3. Strain the custard into a large bowl and stir in the gelatine until dissolved. Set the bowl over iced water to cool the mixture, stirring occasionally until beginning to thicken.

4. Finely chop the rose petals and stir into the cooled mixture with the rosewater. Lightly whip the cream and fold in, using a large metal spoon. Turn into a large glass serving dish or individual glasses and chill for several hours until set.

5. Scatter the raspberries and blueberries over the bavarois. Heat the redcurrant jelly in a saucepan with 75 ml (5 tbsp) water until smooth. Leave to cool, then pour over the fruits. Serve scattered with sugared rose petals.

NOTE: Rosewater varies in strength from brand to brand, and according to freshness. The longer it is stored, the weaker it becomes.

If making the dessert a day in advance, reduce the amount of gelatine to 15 ml (1 tbsp) to ensure it doesn't set too firmly.

SUGARED ROSE PETALS: To make these, brush rose petals with lightly beaten egg white, then dust with caster sugar and leave for at least 1 hour to dry out.

VARIATIONS

Omit the rosewater and petals and use 10 ml (2 tsp) vanilla essence or the finely grated rind of 1 orange instead.

TECHNIQUE

Using a metal spoon fold the lightly whipped cream into the cooled custard.

SYLLABUB WITH POACHED PLUMS

This recipe combines two classic recipes in one. Ripe plums are poached in sweet dessert wine, then topped with a creamy syllabub – lightly infused with fresh rosemary for a distinctive flavour. Let the dessert stand for several hours before serving so that it develops its classic, creamy topping and syrupy, alcoholic base.

SERVES 8

700 g (1½ lb) ripe red plums
50 g (2 oz) caster sugar
175 ml (6 fl oz) dessert wine
2-3 rosemary sprigs
450 ml (¾ pint) double cream

PREPARATION TIME
25 minutes, plus chilling
COOKING TIME
About 12 minutes
FREEZING
Not suitable

350 CALS PER SERVING

1. Quarter the plums, removing the stones. Place the sugar in a saucepan with the wine and heat gently, stirring until the sugar dissolves. Add the plums, cover with a lid and simmer very gently for 5-10 minutes until the plums are softened but not pulpy. (The poaching time will vary, depending on the texture of the plums).

2. Remove from the heat and drain the plums, reserving the syrup. Measure and reserve 200 ml (7 fl oz) of the syrup, making up the quantity with a little extra wine if necessary.

3. Place the rosemary sprigs in a saucepan with 150 ml (¼ pint) of the cream and bring almost to the boil. Remove from the heat and leave to infuse for 15 minutes. Spoon the plums into 8 tall serving glasses.

4. Strain the infused cream into a large bowl and add the remainder. Whip the cream until just holding its shape. Slowly pour in the reserved syrup, whisking well until the mixture is thick enough to leave a trail when the whisk is lifted.

5. Spoon the cream over the plums. Chill the syllabubs for at least 2 hours before serving.

NOTE: The amount of sugar required for poaching the plums will vary, depending on their sweetness. Reduce the sugar if they are very sweet and ripe; add extra if very tart.

VARIATION

Insted of red plums, use yellow dessert plums, or greengages.

TECHNIQUE

Whisk the cream, gradually adding the wine syrup until the mixtures leaves a trail when the whisk is lifted.

SHERRY TRIFLE WITH SOFT FRUIT

Unlike many hastily assembled trifles, a 'real' trifle, based on a homemade sponge and proper custard, is a heavenly treat. For convenience, you can prepare this trifle a day in advance. Keep refrigerated, but remove from the fridge about an hour before serving for optimum flavour.

SERVES 10

SPONGE

125 g (4 oz) self-raising flour

1.25 ml (¼ tsp) baking
  powder

75 g (3 oz) unsalted butter,
  softened

75 g (3 oz) caster sugar

2 eggs

grated rind of 1 orange or
  lemon

CUSTARD

4 egg yolks

15 ml (1 tbsp) cornflour

5 ml (1 tsp) vanilla essence

125g (4 oz) caster sugar

600 ml (1 pint) milk

TO FINISH

60 ml (4 tbsp) raspberry
  conserve

700 g (1½ lb) mixed soft
  fruits (eg raspberries,
  redcurrants, blackberries)

100 ml (3½ fl oz) sherry

90 ml (3 fl oz) freshly
  squeezed orange juice

750 ml (1¼ pints) double
  cream

15 ml (1 tbsp) icing sugar

30 ml (2 tbsp) brandy

finely grated rind of 1 orange

soft fruits and mint sprigs,
  to decorate

PREPARATION TIME
45 minutes, plus cooling
COOKING TIME
40 minutes
FREEZING
Not suitable

660 CALS PER SERVING

1. To make the sponge, grease and line an 18 cm (7 inch) cake tin with grease-proof paper. Preheat the oven to 180°C (350°F) Mark 4. Sift the flour and baking powder into a bowl. Add the butter, sugar, eggs and orange or lemon rind and beat using an electric whisk until pale and creamy. Turn into the prepared tin and bake for about 40 minutes until risen and just firm to the touch. Leave to cool.

2. For the custard, in a bowl whisk the egg yolks, cornflour, vanilla and caster sugar with a little of the milk. Bring the remaining milk to the boil in a saucepan, then pour over the egg mixture, whisk-ing constantly. Return to the saucepan and cook gently, stirring, until thickened enough to coat the back of the spoon; do not boil.

3. Turn the custard into a bowl and cover the surface with greaseproof paper to prevent a skin forming. Leave to cool completely.

4. Split the sponge and sandwich with the raspberry conserve. Cut into pieces and scatter into a glass serving dish. Scatter the fruit over the sponge.

5. Mix together the sherry and orange juice and pour over the fruits and sponge. Cover with the custard.

6. Whip the cream in a bowl with the icing sugar, brandy and orange rind until just peaking. Spread over the custard.

7. Serve decorated with soft fruits and mint or lemon balm.

NOTE: If you haven't time to make your own sponge, use 350 g (12 oz) bought Madeira cake instead.

TECHNIQUE

Cook the custard, without boiling, until it is thick enough to coat the back of the wooden spoon.

CLOTTED CREAM ICE CREAM

Nothing can compare with the flavour of homemade ice cream, particularly this deliciously rich version with its tempting variations. The perfect complement for ripe flavourful summer fruits, serve it in small scoops as it is very rich!

SERVES 4-6

125 g (4 oz) caster sugar
3 egg yolks
10 ml (2 tsp) cornflour
2.5 ml (½ tsp) vanilla
  essence
150 ml (¼ pint) double
  cream
400 g (14 oz) clotted cream
TO SERVE
ripe soft fruits (eg
  raspberries and
  strawberries)

PREPARATION TIME
20 minutes, plus freezing
COOKING TIME
About 10 minutes
FREEZING TIME
About 4 hours

425 CALS PER SERVING

1. Set the freezer to fast-freeze. Put the sugar in a saucepan with 150 ml (¼ pint) water and heat gently, stirring until dissolved. Bring to the boil and boil for 1 minute. Remove from the heat and allow the syrup to cool slightly.

2. Put the egg yolks, cornflour and vanilla essence in a bowl with half of the double cream. Beat until smooth. Heat the remaining double cream in a saucepan with the clotted cream until almost boiling. Pour over the egg yolk mixture, stirring.

3. Return to the saucepan and heat gently, stirring until slightly thickened. Leave to cool, then stir in the syrup.

4. Transfer the ice cream to a freezer-proof container and freeze until semi-frozen, then whisk lightly to break up the ice crystals. Freeze until firm.

5. Transfer the ice cream to the refrigerator about 30 minutes before serving to soften slightly. Serve scooped into individual dishes, with soft fruits.

VARIATIONS

Soft Fruit: Purée 350 g (12 oz) mixed ripe strawberries, raspberries and redcurrants in a blender or food processor, then sieve to remove the pips, Stir into the cream before freezing.

Almond and Amaretto: Reduce the caster sugar to 50 g (2 oz). Stir in 75 g (3 oz) crushed macaroon biscuits and 30 ml (2 tbsp) amaretto liqueur after whisking the partially frozen ice cream.

Creamy Fudge: Reduce the caster sugar to 25 g (1 oz). Grate 75 g (3 oz) cream fudge and stir in after whisking the partially frozen ice cream.

Pear and Ginger: Soak 75 g (3 oz) dried pears in cold water overnight. Drain, chop and add to the sugar syrup. Finely chop 15 g (½ oz) preserved stem ginger and add with the pears after whisking the partially frozen ice cream.

TECHNIQUE

Pour the hot cream onto the egg yolk mixture, stirring constantly.

If you would like further information about the **Good Housekeeping Cookery Club**, please write to:
Penny Smith, Ebury Press, Random House, 20 Vauxhall Bridge Road, London SW1V 2SA.